How to Prevent Lean Implementation Failures

10 Reasons Why Failures Occur

How to Prevent Lean Implementation Failures

10 Reasons Why Failures Occur

Making Companies Globally Competitive Series

Larry Rubrich

WCM Associates
Fort Wayne, Indiana
www.wcmfg.com

How to Prevent Lean Implementations Failures:
10 Reasons Why Failures Occur

By
Larry Rubrich

Copyright 2004 by WCM Associates
All rights reserved
Printed in the United States of America

WCM Associates
P.O. Box 8035
Fort Wayne, IN 46898-8035
260-637-8064
www.wcmfg.com

ISBN # 0-9662906-7-4

Front and rear cover design by:
Robert Howard
rhoward@bookgraphics.com

Book and text design by WCM Associates

Printed and bound by:
Thomson-Shore, Inc.
Dexter, MI
734-426-3939

Layout was completed using Adobe(R) Pagemaker 7.0.
Text typeface is Bookman, 11 point.

Library of Congress Catalog Card Number: 2004111880

*To my wife, Shirley,
and to my children,
Kelly and Todd,
who put up with me
and love me
in spite of my considerable
list of faults.*

Acknowledgments

Acknowledging contributors in a book about what causes "failure" can be a difficult topic. We will, however, attempt to successfully give positive credit to those who helped educate us in this area.

Our North American clients, over the years, have helped us immensely by defining what the measures are along the way of a successful implementation. Since a Lean Enterprise implementation is a culture changing, continuous improvement journey that never ends, the measures we refer to are the road signs that companies use to confirm they are on the desired road. The primary measure tends to be the very traditional measure—profit.

Some Toyota Production System (TPS) purists would say that, if necessary, companies must make a "leap of faith" to commit to the long-term implementation of TPS. The reality of our target market—322,000 companies with 500 or fewer people—is that, if bottom line improvements do not occur in the first 3-6 months after implementation starts, initial excitement and interest can evaporate in the day-to-day heat of running the business and "making the month."

While this environment annoys our "purist side," we are super-advocates of keeping American businesses in America, and have adapted to this environment. Adjusting the Lean implementation schedule to fit the current culture of American companies not only works, but can be accomplished without violating the long-term goals of a TPS implementation. The analogy we would use is from mountain climbing: There are usually several possible paths to successfully get to the top. More about this in the introduction and throughout the book.

Much has been learned also from the classroom sessions that resulted from our relationships with the Milwaukee School of Engineering (MSOE), the Maryland World Class Manufacturing Consortia, and Indiana University-Purdue University Fort Wayne (IPFW). From the thousands of participants in these sessions, we heard about success stories as well as failures. These are invaluable learning experiences.

Contents

Contents

Contents

Contents

Introduction

To get everyone on the same page, let us start by defining World Class/Lean Enterprise as a set of tools and techniques that continuously improve the following business and manufacturing processes:

♦ Safety, quality, productivity, and delivery

While reducing:

♦ Lead times and cost

World Class/Lean Enterprise is implemented through the training, empowerment, and participation of *the entire workforce.*

The goal of World Class Enterprise is to improve and grow the business by being globally competitive.

In this book, Lean Enterprise and World Class Enterprise will be referred to interchangeably. "Lean" happens to be the latest buzz word for these activities, whereas World Class has been around for awhile. If you trace these terms down the "family tree," you will get to the Toyota Production System (TPS). Further down the tree, in the roots, you find American manufacturing from the 1950s, going all the way back to Henry Ford of Ford Motor company.

Industry Week magazine recently reported that 72% of the 884 U.S. companies responding to their survey were in various stages of implementing an improvement strategy such as Lean or World Class manufacturing, Agile manufacturing, Six Sigma, TPS, Theory of Constraints, or others. Of these companies, 75% reported that they had made "no" or just "some" progress toward their World Class manufacturing goals. Only 2% of the companies reported achieving World Class manufacturing status.

Some of the *Industry Week's* survey results may be distorted by what might be called "Lean learning curve effect." Companies with well planned and supported implementation plans can make rapid progress in eliminating waste, improving customer satisfaction, and reducing costs in the first year. If you surveyed these companies and asked how far along they were in their journey to become a World Class Enterprise, they might say 50%. In the second year, these companies continue to make progress eliminating waste and, in addition to eliminating it, also become much better at identifying waste within their company. Surveyed again at the end of their second year, these companies now might report they are 25% of the way there. During the third year, they continue to eliminate waste and continue to get better at identifying it. Surveyed again, now they report they are 10% there. Usually after this low point, the numbers slowly go back up. This is when the company's Lean Champions can get depressed. They begin to wonder if they are making any progress or whether back sliding is occurring. This temporary depression can be prevented by continuously posting good visual records of the company's improvement history (more on this throughout the book).

Why aren't more companies showing significant progress in their goal to become World Class? We have some answers.

As mentioned in the acknowledgments, part of the problem is a reflection on the American business culture. Very few companies in our target market start a Lean/World Class implementation with this vision: We are nicely profitable now, but we believe we may not be competitive in 5-7 years, so we must begin implementing Lean now! This, in the TPS environment, is the ideal time to start a World Class Enterprise (WCE) implementation.

More often companies start this journey because their bottom line is steadily degrading and approaching red ink; they lost a major share of business to a foreign competitor; or their major customer has told them they must improve their quality, improve their delivery, and reduce their lead-time by 75%, or risk losing the business. With a global economy, hundreds of companies face these scenarios on a daily basis. This implementation environment (the business is at risk) is not conducive to looking at the long-term benefits required "by the book" of a WCE implementation. As mentioned in the acknowledgments, "making the month" or "quarter" are still, unfortunately, top priorities in the American business culture.

This short-term view has led to some of the major accounting scandals at companies—especially publicly owned corporations. Some of these companies have created a financial "house of cards" so they can beat Wall Street estimates by a penny each quarter.

Other companies have a more investor palatable way of presenting the cumulative results of their short-term decisions—"restructuring costs."

Recently, the new CEO of a Fortune 200 company was interviewed on television and asked what was the legacy of the retiring/outgoing CEO. The answer: "He began a major company restructuring program." This answer, which was presented in a very positive light, was and is amazing.

Restructuring means that, for some period of time, you took your eye off the customer and the market. You are not agile and flexible in responding to changing customer and market requirements on a daily or weekly basis. Suddenly you find that the company is in dire straits and respond by laying off large numbers of the workforce, closing plants, and/or selling businesses. However, if you are continuously making improvements/adjustments in your business/company/ division everyday, major restructuring changes would be unnecessary. Unfortunately, these improvements/adjustments may not optimize the month's or quarter's results. There is a better way.

> *"You Can't Solve Current Problems With Current Thinking. Current Problems Are The Result Of Current Thinking."*
>
> *Albert Einstein*

What is mentioned here, and further discussed in this book, is the concept of designing and planning the WCE implementation around the current and future company goals that usually are outlined in the company's current budget or business plan. A World Class Enterprise implementation can and should be designed to achieve the company's goals quickly. Unwavering top management support is needed—and positively impacting company results is the way to cement this support. Again, TPS purists would disagree with this formula, but we would be quick to point out that, while we agree and understand that companies need to implement *all the elements of TPS*, it is the *order* of implementation that is being modified to fit the target market.

Understand also that approaching a WCE implementation as a "cost reduction" initiative is a huge mistake. There are many examples of failures resulting from this approach. Cost reduction in a WCE implementation will occur as one of the outcomes of the implementation. Traditional cost reduction programs, often driven by the company's financial people, focus on "head count" reductions or supplier arm twisting to reduce prices, without regard to the supplier's costs.

These are not WCE activities! In fact, they are

detrimental to a WCE implementation because head count reductions create a cycle of fear in the organization that affects morale. The company's best associates may not choose to work in this type of environment. Additionally, to become a World Class company requires World Class suppliers and a win-win supplier relationship with them. Arm twisting is a very short term solution that does not get to the "root cause" (business waste) of the supplier's cost creators and is certainly not win-win. More on this later.

Johnson Controls Inc., has an interesting way of presenting the correct approach to costs with their SQDC slogan (Safety–Quality–Delivery–Cost) as part of their Lean initiative called the Johnson Controls Manufacturing System (JCMS). In the JCMS, the idea was to work from left to right on the SQDC slogan: safety first, then quality, then delivery. If these three were done well, one of the outcomes would be lower costs. Alcan Packaging Corporation (80,000 associates, 50 countries) has a similar approach with their company policy of "EHS First." Their experience/vision is that, as plants approach World Class levels of Environment/Health/Safety, quality and productivity also will be optimized.

So what are the potential bottom-line results of a WCE implementation using the correct approach for your company? The *Industry Week* study also reported that companies with successful implementations reported a 47% improvement in Return on Invested Capital (ROIC) versus the companies who reported "no" or just "some" progress toward their World Class manufacturing goals.

Additionally, these companies enjoyed the positive cash flow of increasing inventory turns brought about by the implementation of WCE tools and techniques.

And what about competing globally using WCE? We are pleased to report that many companies have discovered that the waste elimination tools and techniques of WCE can more than make up the differences in wages. Candy company American Licorice, lawn and garden equipment manufacturer Ariens, and athletic shoe manufacturer New Balance are just a few of the companies that are using WCE techniques to compete globally while manufacturing in the U.S.

Further discussion on how implementing WCE techniques can reduce or eliminate differences in foreign wages is detailed in chapter 10.

The book *Leading Change* by John Kotter is referenced heavily throughout this book. *Leading Change* is a great book on how top management can implement change in their companies—WCE or other types. While *Leading Change* tends to be written about larger companies (>500 people), the concepts are scalable down to the 25 person company. It should be required reading for anyone wishing to successfully implement change in their company.

How to Prevent Lean Implementation Failures: 10 Reasons Why Failures Occur is written in the order of the severity and impact of the reason. Reason #1 and #2 (Chapters 1 and 2) are fatal! Reasons #3 through #10, are costly but survivable, if detected early enough. Reasons #1 through #4 are the most common.

All the reasons tend to overlap or are interrelated, and therefore the ranking presented will be open to discussion and perhaps some disagreement.

Allow none of these reasons to exist in an implementation and all of the bases are covered.

#1 Lack of Top Down Management Support

All successful and sustainable WCE implementations start with top management

Implementing WCE is not a bottom-up, or middle-out implementation. Successful and sustainable implementations are strictly top down! Having said that, it is important to note that top management by itself cannot make a company World Class. Once top management has provided the proper support and foundation for a WCE implementation, companies become World Class when every person in the facility understands why becoming World Class is important to their customers, the company, and ultimately to them. This common goal/mission creates a foundation for everyone to pull in the same direction (teamwork). This lack of a common goal/mission and teamwork is why bottom-up or middle-out implementations cannot change the entire company. Enthusiastic (about WCE) managers or supervisors have been known to make major improvements in their area of control even without the support of top management. Unfortunately, without top management support, sustainability is a problem. The manager gets moved, promoted, or changes jobs, and suddenly everyone remaining is left with the question "Why are we doing this?" To get back into their comfort zone, and with the support of the new manager, the group then puts everything back the way it was before the former manager changed it (more on this throughout the book).

In John Kotter's book, *Leading Change*, he identifies the five change implementation prerequisites that management is responsible for successfully completing, before change can begin:

1. Creating a sense of change urgency

2. Creating/developing a company change guiding coalition or alliance

3. Developing a vision of the required company future state and a strategy to achieve it

4. Communicating the vision and strategy to the entire workforce

5. Creating an environment in the company where associate empowerment can evolve

1. Creating a Sense of Change Urgency

Whether the change is to our personal lives or our business lives, change does not occur without a sense of urgency to do so.

In fact, John Brandt, a contributing editor to *Industry Week* magazine and CEO for The MPI Group, recently noted that the common thread in

> *Management Must Remember:*
> *When problems occur in a business (safety, poor designs, turnover, scrap, low productivity, etc.), 98% of them are a result of the* systems *that company management has put in place—not people. Management must always take responsibility for these problems.*
>
> ♦ *Quit trying to find someone to blame!*
>
> ♦ *Always look for the root cause of problems.*
>
> ♦ *Never accept solutions that are not error proofed!*

the ten-plus years of *Industry Week* "Best Plant" awards is that all of these companies had a "near death" experience.

The reality is that all businesses today are under a tremendous amount of competitive pressure from the global economy. The pre-global economy selling price model was:

Selling Price = Cost + Desired Profit

Rolled up in the cost of the product or service were all the wasteful activities that occurred in the business (scrap, rework, unnecessary overtime, equipment downtime, searching, hunting, looking for stuff, unnecessary motion, reconciliations, supplier invoices, counting inventory, receiving inspection, and on and on and on). This formula has been replaced in the current global economy by:

$$Profit = Selling\ Price - Cost$$

where the selling price is now set by the customer/ consumer. If this is not what is happening in your business today, it's down the street headed your way. Companies today can control profitability only by controlling their costs. WCE is the technique that can accomplish this control.

To create this sense of urgency to change, top management must tell all company associates (that means *everyone*) in a company-wide meeting what the current market conditions are in a professional, non-threatening fashion. Remember, the goal of this communication is to create a sense of urgency, not the potential panic reaction to a threat.

Company associates (98% of them anyway), want to take care of the customer, want the company to be successful, and want their jobs secured in the future. In many cases, associates already recognize the competitive nature of the current business environment. If properly presented, this common mission and common goal provides the basis for everyone pulling together in the same direction (teamwork).

Now that a sense of urgency exists, the tools/ ability for the team to participate in relieving this current sense of urgency must be presented.

2. Creating/Developing a Company Change Guiding Coalition or Alliance

The purpose of this Guiding Coalition or alliance is to help guide the company and the associates through the required changes. Additionally, the Guiding Coalition enhances company-wide, two-way communication in three vital areas of the WCE implementation. These areas are:

♦ Visual and verbal updates to the entire company on the status of the WCE implementation

♦ Honest feedback from all areas of the company on how the implementation is proceeding. Successes as well as suggested improvements.

♦ Making and communicating WCE implementation course adjustments along the way. These adjustments can occur for three reasons:

1. Most companies are only successful with 70-80% of their improvement implementation efforts. This means that companies will try certain improvement activities that will be unsuccessful. This learning experience may force the company to adjust its implementation course.

2. Customer requirements and market conditions can change over the years that a WCE implementation can take.

3. Company business and marketing strategies can change over time.

With these purposes in mind, members of the Guiding Coalition must include/represent:

♦ All levels within the organization

♦ People who are trusted by their peers

♦ Good communicators and team players

♦ Individuals with a strong desire to participate in securing the future

♦ A good mix of both leaders and managers. Leaders drive the changes and managers control the process. Too many managers on this team result in team members from the lower levels in the organization eventually not being heard.

3. Developing a Vision of the Company Future State and a Strategy to Achieve

Top company management, with their high-level view of customers and markets, must develop a visual picture and verbal description of what the company must look like at some point in the future (3-5-10 years) to insure that the company is still competitive and still in business. This vision must include people and processes, as well as products and services. The reality is this: becoming a World Class company by itself does not guarantee a company's future. The company must still produce a product or service that customers want. For example: if a company was the World Class producer of buggy whips or steam engines, would it still be in business? Probably not.

The strategy to become World Class consists of two parts:

♦ WCE to eliminate waste and efficiently run the processes that provide what the customer is willing to pay for (value-added processes).

♦ A sales/marketing plan which always is in touch with the "voice of the customer."

4. Communicating the Vision and Strategy to the Entire Workforce

This is where American management fails miserably! Creating the vision and strategy can be done successfully—even superbly. Somehow, however, it is believed that if six or seven of the top managers know what the plan is, it will become a reality. To use a football analogy, it's like the quarterback going into the huddle and telling only the wide receiver and the halfback what the play is and then expecting the play to be successful. The *entire team* must know the play to be successful.

We are fully expecting our people to do the right thing, and they will beyond our expectations, but we must communicate to them what the customer wants them to do.

This discussion is continued in Chapter 2

which is dedicated to the power of good play/plan communication.

5. Creating an Environment Where Associate Empowerment Can Evolve

Yes, *evolve* is the correct word. Associate empowerment is an evolutionary process, not revolutionary!

All the tools and techniques of WCE are designed to eliminate business waste. Like tools in a tool box, each tool has a waste identification or elimination specialty. Unfortunately, the WCE tools are in a "locked" tool box unless associates are empowered to open the box. This is a key point. In the above example of communicating the plan to only 6 or 7 managers, these 6 or 7 managers could make some changes and improvements in the next 12 months. Could these improvements make the company globally competitive? Probably not.

Instead of just communicating to the 6 or 7 managers, communicate to the entire workforce— say 400 people. Communicate the company's vision and strategy, teach 400 people the WCE tools and techniques, and ask them to make small improvements in their work area everyday. After 12 months of this, the company has now made huge improvements.

The company may not be globally competitive yet, but if you stand on a ladder, you can see World Class from there!

The problem is that this level of empowerment

and participation takes years to develop because of the evolutionary nature of empowerment. This means that creating this environment must start today!

But what are the elements of an empowered environment? They are:

♦ Associates are recognized as the most valuable resource. World Class companies recognize that their associates can differentiate them from the competition. While the competition may be able to duplicate their facilities and equipment, they may not be able to duplicate the participation and motivation of their people.

♦ Teamwork is utilized throughout the organization.

♦ Decision making is delegated to the lowest possible levels in the company.

♦ Openness, initiative, and risk-taking are promoted.

♦ Accountability, credit, responsibility, and ownership are shared. Ownership means psychological ownership, which is far more important to empowerment than just stock certificate ownership. Psychological ownership develops as a result of associates feeling like the 100 square feet they work in everyday is "their part of the business."

A better understanding of what empowerment

is can be developed also by knowing the barriers to empowerment. The common thread through all these barriers is a lack of communication. The barriers are:

♦ Lack of trust

♦ Poor communication—can lead to lack of clear expectations, lack of trust, and fear

♦ Fear—people fear the unknown and therefore resist change

♦ Lack of training—inadequate training leads to confusion, frustration, and anger

♦ Lack of measurements—align all company systems to the vision. First, you must measure the current performance of any activity that you wish to improve. No measurement—no improvement, or said another way: If you don't measure a process, you can't understand it; if you don't understand it, you can't improve it. Second, to implement WCE, you must revise the company's associate evaluation systems, promotion systems, pay increase methods, and bonus systems to support WCE implementation goals. There cannot be mixed messages in any company systems. For example: people who do not support WCE won't get promoted.

Other Areas of Required Top Management Support

WCE Kickoff Meeting

The initial kickoff meeting, which includes creating the sense of urgency and discussion of the company's vision and strategies, must come from the top manager in the organization. There cannot be any question about the company's direction, and the only way people can be assured of that is to hear it from the top person.

To prevent rumors from developing and spreading, these meetings should include all company associates and should occur in as short a time period as possible.

This communication should include a deployment plan and timetable so company associates know when they will become involved.

No Layoff Policy

A "no layoff policy" as a result of WCE improvements must be implemented on day one. This does not mean that if the company loses a major customer or the economy goes into a recession that layoffs cannot occur. It does mean that no one goes out the door as a result of the major productivity and other improvements that occur with WCE. Only normal attrition can be used to reduce the number of associates.

There is a very practical reason for this. WCE is a people-based improvement activity. Eighty percent of the ideas and improvements that occur in a company's World Class journey will come from the people in the company. If people think that they or other associates will be laid off as a result of their ideas, there will not be any more participation in making improvements.

So, what do companies do in this transitional period between being a traditional manufacturer and growing the business as a result of the improved competitiveness that moving toward WCE brings? First, they "in-source" jobs, operations, and material that had previously been out-sourced to suppliers. Second, the extra people are moved into additional/other WCE activities. This accelerates the amount of improvements that can be made. Some companies do both—"in-source" jobs and move people into WCE activities. Third, as a result of customer needs to bring new products to the market rapidly, the extra people are moved into new product development.

The Power of WCE—A Real Life Example

The American Licorice Company reduced this transitional period by almost immediately converting quality and productivity improvements that their associates made into product price reductions to their brokers and customers. Improved visibility as a candy supplier and improved sales were the result.

Understand that this no-layoff policy only applies to the WCE implementation. If the company loses a major customer or the economy goes into recession, layoffs may be necessary to protect the survival of the company.

Summary—Reason #1

Lack of top management support for a WCE implementation can be an extremely costly, and if left unaccomplished, a fatal mistake. Management must prepare the foundation for this change to WCE, and then let the associates make the company World Class.

#2 Lack of Communication

Of the eight types of business waste:

> **Scrap/Rework/Repack/Recook/Corrections/Reconciliations**
>
> **Transportation**—Material handling or information "hand-offs"
>
> **Associate Motion**—Non-value-added time such as looking for, searching, obtaining items such as prints, tools, materials, memos, files, reports, invoices
>
> **Associate Waiting Time**—Non-value-added time such as waiting for materials, instructions, the supervisor, an e-mail, or a phone call
>
> **Inventory**—Raw, work-in-process, finished
>
> **Overproduction**—Producing more than the customer ordered
>
> **Overprocessing**—Doing more than what the customer is willing to pay for
>
> **Underutilized Human Resources**—The lack of involvement and participation of all the members of the workforce

the worst and most prevalent form of waste in American business is number eight: Underutilized Human Resources.

People—Our Most Underutilized Asset

It is interesting to note that the Japanese only recognize the first seven types of business waste, since fully utilizing their workforces has been a part of their culture at least since the end of World War II, when the belief "none of us have anything so let's all work together to get something" was prevalent. Others might add that "company" unions and a homogeneous population add to their ability to form teams and have everyone pulling in the same direction.

For American business, we would propose that the other seven forms of waste exist in huge amounts because of #8. The rest of this chapter explains how this can possibly be true.

We Say We Want Teamwork, But . . .

When the top management person in a company, the CEO, President, or Plant Manager, is asked whether team work is important and required within the organization, the answer 99% of the time is yes, absolutely! This answer flows quickly and easily from these managers. The follow-up questions for the 99% are these: Does that mean that all the members of your workforce, from machine operator in the plant (or the window teller in a bank) to the staff level managers have a copy of the company's playbook (business plan or budget)? Does every associate in your operation know what they must do hourly/daily/weekly to achieve the plan and keep the company successful now and in the future?

The reaction to these questions is in three parts. First, there is a question mark look; second, stunned silence and some embarrassment at the recognition of the issue; third, admission that all of their associates do not know what the plan is and do not have a copy of the playbook. Then, there is discussion on how to move forward in this area.

Why are managers saying they want organizational team work, yet there is no ongoing activity or plan to achieve it? Several reasons:

♦ Many top managers today were raised/ trained/developed when "teaming" was not important. Now that teams are essential to competing, these managers can "talk it" but they can't "walk it" organizationally.

♦ Or the worst case, these same managers see the "team" as themselves and the 6 or 7 people that report to them—with "the company wouldn't exist without us," attitude and "why doesn't everyone appreciate us for that?"

♦ Or the second worst case, the top managers see the team as the management group only. Hourly associates, whether they are nonunion or union, are not considered part of the team even though 90% of all value-adding processes, (activities the customer is willing to pay for and where profits are created) are completed by this group.

In a recent visit to a small company, it was

suggested to the CEO that it was appropriate to get the company's associates' opinion
on a particular WCE issue. This CEO then
proceeded to schedule a meeting with his
22 managers, almost as if the people out in
the factory didn't exist. It was disappointing.

In the previous chapter (Reason #1), it was
mentioned that top management, by itself, cannot
make a company World Class. Top management
starts to build the proper support and foundation
for a WCE implementation by using the five change
pre-implementation steps listed on page 10.

To repeat Step #4 (Communicating the Vision
and Strategy to the Entire Workforce) is where
American business fails miserably. The remain-
der of this chapter discusses the power of good
communication in making your company World
Class and how the lack of communication can prevent teamwork and the empowerment vital to a
successful WCE implementation.

Human Nature and Change

People have a natural human reaction to
change which is shown in Figure 2-1. Good two-
way communication about the change, which must
include how it will affect the company's customers, the company, and the individual associate,
can cause interest to begin in the change (bypassing rumors, fear, resistance and resentment). Left
under communicated with no scheduled and direct follow-up communication, change can cause
rumors, fear, resistance, and resentment. These
organizational cancers can be very costly, in both

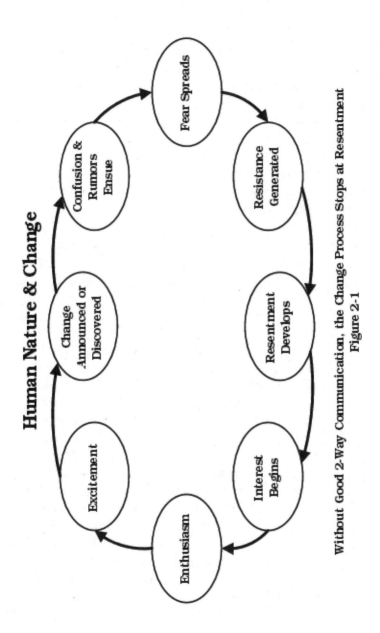

Human Nature & Change

Fear Spreads

Confusion & Rumors Ensue

Resistance Generated

Change Announced or Discovered

Resentment Develops

Excitement

Interest Begins

Enthusiasm

Without Good 2-Way Communication, the Change Process Stops at Resentment

Figure 2-1

financial and human terms, to an organization.

People can embrace change in terms of inter-est, enthusiasm, and excitement only if there are high levels of two-way communication in the or-ganization. Two-way communication can drive fear out of organizations. While a sense of urgency is essential, fear can be paralyzing.

When the WCE implementation change is an-nounced, it must be followed immediately by (and in this order of importance):

1. Management is visible and available to thoroughly discuss the change on all shifts for the first few days after the change an-nouncement.

2. Follow-up meetings to discuss questions. The real issue is that not all the questions will come out during the change announce-ment meeting. People need time to think about it. Family members will have ques-tions that require answers. Left unan-swered, all these questions will be given answers in the "rumor mill." The rumor mill, which never seems to create favorable answers, supports answers which heighten fear, resistance, and resentment. The key is to provide enough timely communication to put the rumor mill out of business. This has the effect of bypassing the confusion (ru-mors), fear, resistance, and resentment parts of the change continuum. People go from change announcement to interest in the change.

3. Telephone hot lines, check stuffers repeating the details of the change meeting. Questions submitted through idea or suggestion boxes are other ways of improving communication on this issue and in general.

Communicate, communicate, communicate. Communication is empowering. Communication eliminates wasteful human mental activity: rumors, fear, resistance, resentment, and substitutes the value-added mental activities of understanding, knowledge, focus, and motivation.

Unfortunately, most managers don't understand the power of communication and its role in teamwork, and therefore, they under communicate. In most organizations, this under communication is not by 40, 50, or 75%—but by magnitudes of 500 or 1000%.

Communication, Teamwork, & Productivity

There are four elements that must be in place for teamwork to occur in an organization. These elements, in order, are:

1. *High levels of two-way communication throughout the organization.* Communication can dramatically increase productivity by keeping everyone aware of the mission, vision, goals, and strategy of the organization. In World Class companies, top managers spend as much as 40% of their time communicating this vital information to their organization.

2. *Team members with diverse backgrounds.* Diversity helps teams approach problems from a variety of angles, thus ensuring an effective, robust solution. Diversity also means hourly and salary associates can be on the same team.

3. *Common purpose, motivated by mission.* A strongly developed vision and mission for the organization helps all team members make the right decisions and saves time in the decision-making process. One has only to ask "Does this decision support the goals of the organization?"

4. *Common goals, common measurements.* Teamwork is enhanced when all team members understand the goals of the team and the organization; Common measurements, understood by everyone, are used to assess the progress made.

Several universities have done studies on what factors in the workplace produce the highest levels of productivity. These studies discovered that only two factors were required to produce the highest levels of workplace productivity. When high levels of job satisfaction and high levels of two-way communication existed, productivity was at it peak. A chart, showing the results of these studies is shown in Figure 2-2.

How do we define these factors? High levels of two-way communication in the studies agrees with the definition above. It means that everyone knows what's going on in the organization, and they feel comfortable and confident with their organizational knowledge. Rumors about the company are eliminated or at least minimized.

Level of Productivity	Two-way Comunication Level	Job Satisfaction Level
1 (highest)	High	High
2	High	Low
3	Low	High
4 (lowest)	Low	Low

Factors Affecting Workplace Productivity
Figure 2-2

High levels of "job satisfaction" means that the associate or associates are in their "dream" job. If they could pick any job, it would be the one they have.

Here's the rub. Other studies of the American workforce found that only 17% of American workers are in their "dream job." This means that the highest levels of workplace productivity can be achieved with only 17% of the workforce. So what do we do for the other 83% of our workforce?

Most managers get this part wrong. When given the choice of picking what level of factors determine the second highest level of productivity (affecting 83% of the workforce), managers generally pick low levels of two-way communication and high levels of job satisfaction, which is actually the third level of productivity. Why does this occur? Primarily because managers find it easy to blame the people: "They applied for a job they really didn't like, how were we supposed to know?", instead of understanding that 98% of the problems in business are related to the management created "systems," and look at the systems first (the system of communication, in this example).

High levels of two-way communication help create teamwork and improve company productivity with no capital equipment investment. Who said we needed new equipment and a new IT system to be competitive?

The Power of Communication—A Real Life Example

In 1993, United Technologies Automotive (UTA) owned a facility in Howe, Indiana. The facility produced automotive interiors. On May 1st, I arrived at the facility as the new plant manager to find the following conditions:

♦ 250 people, unionized facility

♦ The previous month, the plant lost $400,000.00 (and had been losing money every month)

♦ Plant was operating at a quoted efficiency of 42%. In UTA's world, 85% was what was expected from the plants. At this point, the Howe plant was at 49% of where the corporation wanted it to be. Stated another way, if we were supposed to produce 10,000 pieces per day, we were only producing 4,900 pieces.

♦ Premium freight charges, previous 12 months, $68,000.00

♦ Lost time accidents for previous 12 months = 32, Workers Compensation charges for 1993 = $155,000.00

Basically, the understanding between the corporation and the management group was that if the plant was not operating profitably in 12 months, it would be closed. We didn't feel threatened by this understanding—it was a fact of business that we understood—because companies are in business to make money. It did, though, create a sense of urgency for change.

What We Changed

♦ The first all-associate monthly meeting was held on May 7th. We wanted to share financials with the associates and it took us 5 days to close April. This was a three shift operation, so we conducted two meetings, first and third shifts together and then second shift (optimum is one meeting, because everyone should hear the exact same presentation, and the exact same questions and answers). Attendance at these meetings was mandatory. They were held monthly like clockwork.

In the first meeting, we laid out the status of the plant and the financials in a non-threatening manner. No one outside the management group had seen the financials before. It took some explaining. We told everyone that we were in this together and that the key was teamwork—we would either win as a team—or lose as a team. There would be no individual winners or losers.

It is interesting to note a comment that was overheard from a company supervisor after the first company meeting which was about an hour in length: "What a waste of an hour, we could have been making parts all that time!" My thought, "Yeah, and at 42% efficiency!" Sometime later this supervisor made the comment that the problem with the plant was that all the shop floor people were stupid. Shortly after that comment, this supervisor was given the opportunity to contribute at another company. More information on WCE implementation "brick walls" disguised as supervisors/managers is in Reason #3.

♦ On day two, we discovered that it was difficult for the production associates to communicate with the rest of the facility. The plant was long, narrow, and divided into three sections by walls. If a particular production line or manufacturing cell had a problem (for example, they needed more raw material, had a quality problem, or one of their machines had broken down) they had two choices. They could go to a supervisor's desk and page the person over the PA system (which some people didn't like to do), or they could wander around the plant looking for the appropriate person. While this person was looking for help (all motion waste), the line was generally not running (waiting waste)—all due to poor communication.

To improve communication between the production operators and the rest of the facility, we installed Andon or signalling lights like the ones shown in Figure 2-3. This is nothing more than a column of different colored lights where each light has a specific meaning and each column is numbered to represent different production areas cells. A green light indicated the production cell is running and meeting the customer's production and quality requirements. A red light indicated the production cell is down for a machine or quality problem that the team can't fix themselves and immediate assistance is needed. This light was wired so an alarm rang when it was turned on. A three person response team (Quality, Maintenance, and Supervision) was set up to go to the particular cell number on the Andon display. Only a member of the response team could turn the audible alarm off. A blue light indicated the production cell needed raw material delivered or parts picked up. An amber or yellow light was the signal that a supervisor was needed

Andon Light System
Figure 2-3

in the area. The white light, which the teams nicknamed the "brag light," meant the team had implemented an improvement which allowed the production cell to run quality parts at a rate higher than the "standard" rate.

♦ One of the rules in WCE is that you must first standardize and then measure any activity you wish to improve. At the UTA-Howe plant, we set up production boards, like the one shown in Figure 2-4, in all production areas and cells. Production boards like these generally invoke fear in the production associates because they are typically used by traditional managers as tools to beat people up. In WCE, they are used strictly as communication tools.

The board shown in Figure 2-4 was used as follows. Each hour the customer require-ment for this particular part was 38 pieces. If after the first hour, the team produced 38 pieces, the team would post the 38 pieces on the board for that hour along with the total for the shift which, after one hour, was also 38 pieces. Let's say during the second hour the team had a quality problem that reduced their productivity to 30 pieces. On the board they would post 30 pieces for the second hour and now, after two hours, the total is 68 pieces. The team was also responsible for noting in the "comments" column what prevented them from doing what the customer required that hour—producing 38 pieces. It was then management's responsibility to review the

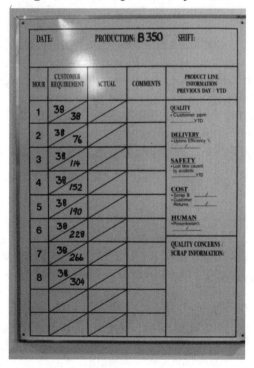

Production/Measurement Board
Figure 2-4

boards to determine what problems the teams needed their help solving. When cells were not producing to the customer's requirements, it was a problem for the entire company team.

Information was collected hourly (real time is even better) on the production boards because, if the team fell behind because of a problem, it was possible for them to make adjustments and catch up. Without the production boards, the cell team and the rest of the company had no idea where they were in their schedule.

♦ To raise the awareness of safety problems in the plant, a safety incentive system was started. OSHA will caution companies about using safety incentive systems because they believe that people will be tempted not to report accidents if it will hurt the incentive system. This is a legitimate concern that must be addressed in the development of the system.

During the second plant meeting (June), the plant manager stood next to a 25" color television (not a big deal today, but it was huge in 1993) and said that we would raffle off one TV for every month during which there were no lost time accidents. There was one lost time accident in June, and then the plant went two years without a lost time accident.

♦ To help develop company-wide team work, we also implemented what was called "Adopt-a-Cell." Each management person was asked to adopt one of the production cells. The goal was to provide visible, physical, verbal, purchasing, roadblock breaking, or what ever kind of support the production teams needed. It was a way of showing that we were all in it together. Management people run machines, attended daily cell meetings, and purchased needed cell supplies and equipment. The plant's financial controller spent two weeks on second shift with the team from cell #7. For most of the management group, it was a valuable shop floor learning experience.

Four to Six Months Later—More Change

As we learned to communicate and teamwork grew throughout the plant, the following additional changes were implemented:

♦ We held daily "start of the shift production meetings" with all cells. The purpose of these meetings was to communicate schedules, to review cell problems and status of solutions, and to review the previous day's performance. Meeting length was 10 minutes maximum.

♦ Customer quality issues became the responsibility of the team that manufactured the product. When a customer called and said they had a problem with our product and needed someone to come to their facility, members of the team that produced it went to the customer's plant. This wasn't done to punish or be punitive to the teams; it was done to put the team members, who were the process experts and in the best position to fix a product problem, in direct face-to-face contact with their unhappy customer. It was pleasing to note that none of the teams were required to go to the customer twice about the same problem.

♦ The plant manager stopped giving customer tours. When customers or prospective customers wanted a plant tour, the plant manager would escort the customer to the first manufacturing cell where the customer was handed over to the cell team leader. The team leader would introduce the customer to the associates who worked in the cell and show the customer how the cell processed material. When that cell tour was complete, the team leader would escort the customer to the next cell's team leader. At the end of the tour, the plant manager met the customer at the other side of the plant.

This system worked great. Customers liked it, and as it turned out, the cell associate were some of the best sales people around. It also gave the production associates the proper respect for their knowledge, skills, and contributions.

♦ When we had supplier quality problems, our suppliers had to answer to the production cells also. Suppliers had to be taught that their customer, the people they had to satisfy, was the cell that used their product, not the purchasing department.

Celebrations Along the Way

Celebrating improvements along the way is very much a part of a WCE. They don't have to be expensive celebrations, or take a lot of planning or time. We celebrated with donuts, hats, "T" shirts, cookouts (even in the winter), and jackets. It was a way of having some fun and saying "thank you" to the entire team.

Sometimes we get so focused on what needs to be done, that we lose sight of what has been accomplished. Celebrations allow us to look back at the progress so far and thereby re-energize our efforts.

Often we were accused of making up reasons to celebrate, but here is a list of improvements we used to celebrate:

♦ Every 10% improvement in company effi-ciency

♦ When an individual cell's performance achieved 100% (we mean 100%, not the 85% UTA would have accepted)

♦ Every time a new white Andon light was on (the record was eight at one time)

♦ The first year we went without a lost-time accident (and saved $105,000.00)

What About Results?

♦ We started our journey in May; by October of that year the plant efficiency was at 65% (a 55% improvement)

♦ November of that year was our first profitable month

♦ By February of the following year the plant was at 80% efficiency (a 90% improvement)

♦ In April we made a $186,000.00 profit (a $586,000.00 turn around from the previous May)

♦ In July the plant efficiency hit 100% (a 138% improvement and the only plant in the division ever to achieve this level of performance)

. . . And the Most Remarkable Part of the Results!

We went from 42% company-wide efficiency to 80% and all that was done was to develop 2-way communications and promote teamwork! It wasn't until we reached 80% that we had the nerve to ask the corporation for money to spend on improvements.

It is important to note that the productivity increases shown in the above example were not achieved because people were working harder or faster. They were working smarter. Working smarter means eliminating or reducing people's wasteful activities (scrap, rework, machine down-time, machine setup time, searching, hunting, looking for people or things, etc.) and substitut-ing value-added activities (activities the customer will pay for) such as more throughput (more on this in Reason #5). People would say the morale was much higher and the work environment less stressful when this plant was producing at 100% versus the initial 42%.

Managers often look at results like these and make excuses such as, "these were special cir-cumstances", or "you don't understand our busi-ness, we're different." Nonsense, all nonsense! These results are available in any business where the leaders and managers are fully committed to creating a sense of urgency, 2-way communica-tion, and teamwork. The managers that make ex-cuses always find it easier to blame "the people" than to look inward at their own performance.

Not convinced that huge improvements in pro-ductivity are available in your business? Do the "Pie Analysis" of your business (office, factory, or both) as shown in Reason #10 and find out for yourself.

Considerations in Developing a Communications Plan

The power of any communications plan comes from people understanding the plan so they can take action in their area. A good plan includes both visual and verbal communication (we like a 50-50 split). Verbal communication must be simple and should not include jargon. A good test is this: if you presented the plan to a family member (assuming he or she is not intimately knowledgeable about the business), would the family member understand? Use metaphors, analogies, and plenty of examples. Use multiple forums to present the information in both verbal and visual formats: cell or area meetings, bulletin boards, check stuffers, information centers, company newsletters, etc. If a P&L is presented at company meetings (highly suggested), don't let the CFO prepare a 50-line P&L. Shorten it to the highlights, maybe 10 lines. Show the line items that the team can affect. Understand that the first time you show it, 90% of the team will not understand it. Repetition of the message, over time, and good two-way communication (questions) will develop understanding.

In a WCE implementation, all communication is worthless unless management is prepared to back it up by being the models, examples, and leaders of the change we are communicating. The days of "do as I say, not as I do," are long gone. Tom Peters, noted author, said it well, "they watch your feet, not your lips." Management can destroy a WCE implementation by showing people that these activities are "someone else's" job.

There is only one thing for sure in every WCE implementation. Management will make some mistakes along the way. Because a WCE implementation cannot be done with a "cookie cutter," it is difficult to handle every situation perfectly. Two rules: First, deal with these mistakes or difficult issues immediately. Don't let the rumor mill or the WCE nay sayers have time to get cranked up with their "spin" on the subject—management credibility is at stake. Second, deal with these issues openly and honestly. The team is not expecting the top managers to be perfect—but they are demanding honesty and integrity.

Monthly Company Meetings

At a minimum, monthly "all associate company meetings" are a must in a WCE implementation. Some World Class companies, understanding the power of good two-way communication, actually have them every two weeks. To this monthly requirement, we often get "push-back" from managers. "We do quarterly meetings, isn't that good enough?" No! This reminds us of the supervisor who thought the company meeting was a waste of time when we were at 42% efficiency. By the way, company meetings continued occurring like clockwork even after the plant was at 100% efficiency. Again, the reason for having at least monthly meetings is very practical. Remember that the purpose of the communication plan is to provide information so people can take action on it in their area (the 400 people all pulling in the same direction). If it is reported in the quarterly company meeting that the company had a poor quarter, and this is the first time people have heard about it, just how is everyone supposed to help prevent that from occurring? It's too late! The reason we would like "real time" performance information about how a cell or the company is doing, is so the team can make immediate adjustments and prevent the poor month and/or quarter.

Visual Communication

Communication is the key to developing teams and making them effective and successful. Communication is important among team members, between management and the team, and between the team and other members of the organization. Speaking is one way to share information. However, we do not always have time to get everyone together and tell them what is going on. There are faster, more effective ways to get the message across.

Visual communication uses specific methods and techniques to provide fast, two-way communication between teams, shifts, coworkers, and management. Visuals provide information that can be used to compare the goals of the team and the company so that performance can be measured. Focus the visual communication on the performance of the group compared to its goals.

Visual communication can be used anywhere in the organization. For example, visuals can show the performance of the plant against its productivity goals, the performance of a work cell against its quality and productivity objectives, and how well a specific part of the process is performing.

Visual communication may be used to identify missing tools or materials and is extremely effective in pull systems. The only limit to the effectiveness of visual communication is a team's creativity.

Figures 2-5 through 2-7 are examples of activities that are typically visually displayed.

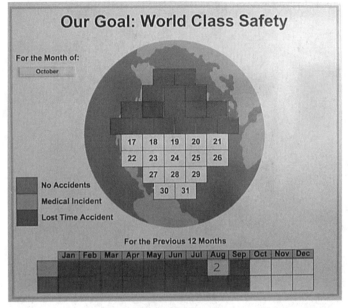

Safety Measurement Board
Figure 2-5

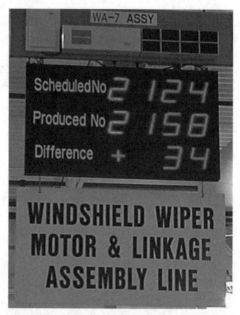

Real Time Production Board
Figure 2-6

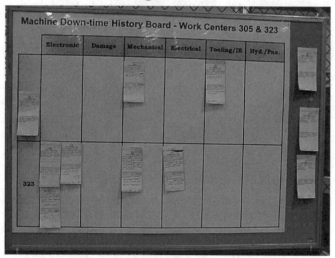

Machine Downtime History Board
Figure 2-7

Measuring Communication Effectiveness

Like all WCE activities, if we want to know whether we are improving, we must measure. Several methods:

♦ Tom Peters uses the expression "Management By Walking Around" (MBWA). We like this as a way of measuring communication effectiveness when it is combined with randomly asking associates about their knowledge of information that has been communicated to them. Remember to begin all questions with what, when, how, or why so the question cannot be answered with a simple yes or no.

♦ Some companies also hire outside services to perform associate surveys about communication.

♦ The amount of rumors travelling around the company is also a measure—as communication effectiveness goes up, rumors go down. Start your monthly company meetings by asking the question, "has anyone heard any good rumors lately?"

♦ The type and amount of questions that are asked at the all-associate meetings are also a measure of both the level of two-way communication in the organization and communication effectiveness. When any associate can openly and honestly ask really tough questions, questions that make top management squirm a little bit, two-way communication is probably in place. When associates are asking questions about things management has previously communicated, the effectiveness of the previous communication can be questioned.

♦ World Class companies measure the effectiveness of their visual communication by using visitors to their company. Their goal: If a visitor can tell what's going on in the company, certainly the company has visually communicated enough that the associates will know what's going on.

Summary—Reasons #1 and #2

Reasons #1 and #2 are fatal errors for a WCE implementation. It's not a matter of picking and choosing what the company would like to do, or what's easy to do. The concern should be, since this is not a cookie cutter approach: Is there an element of Reason #1 or #2 that should be added to cover a particular aspect of our business? Remember, lacking either of these support elements, WCE will irretrievably end up with other company initiatives in the "program of the month" graveyard.

Communication Exercise

There is a rule in the world of advertising that says a customer must see an advertisement four times before the customer understands the ad. The four-times rule also applies to how we communicate in our business and is why we advocate communicating the same information through multiple forums and venues.

To perform this exercise, hand five sheets of blank paper to each participant. Have them number the sheets 1-5 in the upper right corner of the sheet. Tell the participants that you are going to read them a series of instructions and five statements. After each statement, you will ask them a question or questions. Because this is an example of the problems with one-way communication, no questions from the participants are allowed. They are to write the answers on sheet #1. When they have answered all 5 questions, they will turn sheet #1 face down and take sheet #2. The same instructions, statements, and questions will be read again. This is completed a total of four times.

One-Way Communication & the Four-Times Rule

Write #1 in the upper left corner of the paper and answer these questions:

1. In this list of names—George, John, David, Adam, James, Grace—which names begin with a J?

Underneath your answer write the numbers 2A and 2B.

2. Suppose you were given these directions: Go to Room 315 and look in the lower right-hand drawer and bring me all the boxes of pencils that are left there.

   a. Would you look in the right or left-hand drawer?

   b. Would you go to room 5-3-1, 3-1-5 or 1-5-3?

Now write the number 3.

3. Answer true or false to this: In the list of words: BEE, SEE, FREE, GLEE, FLEA, ME, the second word mentioned is FREE.

Now write the number 4.

4. Your spouse asks you to bring home meat, milk, cheese, bread. You bring home milk, peas, bread, and meat. What did you forget?

Now write the number 5.

5. You are the driver of a school bus. At the first stop thirteen children get on. At the second stop five children get on and two get off. At the next stop, eight children get on. At the next stop, four more get on and one sneaks off. How old is the bus driver?

Participant #	Test #1	Test #2	Test #3	Test #4
1				
2				
3				

Example Communication Test Sheet
Figure 2-8

Scoring the Exercise

After the above statements and questions have been read four times, the facilitator will give the answers:

1. 20 points for both James and John.

2a. 10 points for right drawer.

  b. 10 points for room 315

3. 20 points for False—second word is SEE

4. 20 points for cheese

5. 20 points if they wrote their own age.

Participants record their scores for each round on page #5 as shown in this example:

1) 20%

2) 60%

3) 80%

4) 100%

All participants then turn in page 5 to the facilitator who posts all the scores on a white board or flip chart in the format shown in Figure 2-8.

Discussion topics:

1. Did anyone score 100% the first time even though everyone knew they would be tested?

2. Did everyone score 100% by the fourth time? Why or why not?

3. Why would allowing two-way communication improve the scores?

4. What are the implications of this exercise for your organization? How many times do you repeat the message?

#3 Lack of Middle Management/Supervisor Buy-in

An Organization's Response to Change

Studies on how people respond to organizational change have been made by W. Edwards Deming, Tom Peters, and others. These studies discovered that there is a reaction to change by the people in the organization that is called the 10-80-10 rule. A chart illustrating this rule is shown in Figure 3-1.

The chart shows three levels of response to change in the organization. The first level is the high performers. These are the people who, when told once what the new change and plan is, are in their work areas trying to implement the change. High performers need only to be supplied with a company contact person for questions about the new plan and change as questions develop.

The second level is the solid performers of the silent majority. The company needs the support of this group to change. There are some skeptics is this group, but in general they will take a wait-and-see approach. They require an opportunity to ask questions and express their concerns. They expect information about why the change is necessary, what is expected from them, and when is

% of Company	Perfomance Level	What To Do
10%	Top performers, hard workers, will always do the right thing	Reward
80%	Solid performers, silent majority, must have their support for change	Communicate, communicate, communicate
10%	Unconcerned about the company's future, don't want to change, say we've always done it this way, no participation, no ownership	The company's future is at risk with these people as part of the organization

10-80-10 Rule for Organizational Change
Figure 3-1

it going to happen. They need convincing that this is not another "program of the month." This group adjusts to the change over time, with the time frame being up to 12 months for some members of the group. Some members of this group should be on the Guiding Coalition. Other members of the silent majority should be asked to participate early on in WCE improvement activities such as kaizen events. This is generally a very positive experience, and will accelerate the acceptance and support for the change.

We hesitate to call the third level the poor performers because there are good performers in this group. Typically, these are the gripers and complainers who don't want to accept change and wonder why we can't keep doing things like we did in the 80s. Poor attitude is what puts some of the good performers in this group. Others in this group are truly poor performers and could care less whether the company succeeds or fails. These are the 2% you wished worked for the competition.

Brick Walls Disguised as Supervisors/ Middle Managers

Included, but not immediately recognizable in the third level, are some supervisors and middle managers. They are not immediately recognizable because, during the initial communications, meetings, and training about WCE, they are all shaking their heads, saying "yes, yes, we as a company need to do this." Unfortunately, when they get back to their work area or out on the factory floor, they revert to their "command and control" style of supervision (which management probably taught them years ago) and now it's "no, no, just do as I've always told you to do."

It is wishful thinking to believe that these "brickwalls," disguised as a supervisor or middle manager, don't exist in all organizations that have been around for a while. Our experience has been, and it is supported again by the literature, that if people-barriers occur in a WCE implementation, they will be management people.

The one caveat that we would add to this is that in unionized facilities, management and the union *must* agree on the WCE implementation need and strategy first *before it is announced or introduced.* The point: change is difficult—and when an associate goes to his supervisor or the shop steward with a question about the WCE implementation, the answer needs to be the same.

The John Deere Story

In the early 90s, John Deere's top management had the excellent foresight and vision to understand that they would need to implement World Class manufacturing techniques in their facilities if they were to stay competitive in the very tough farm equipment business. By our measures and understanding, Deere management did all the right things. They had meetings early on with their UAW union so that both management and the UAW were on the same page. They did the proper amount of communication and training.

About a year into the implementation, Deere management was disappointed by what little improvement progress had been made. An investigation revealed that two levels of Deere management, supervisors and middle managers, who in the meetings and training were saying yes to World Class, would later go back to their work areas and say "no, no, we are doing it the way we've always done it."

To quickly get the implementation back on track, Deere eliminated those two levels of management on their organizational chart. In some cases they made UAW members team leaders to fill in for the missing supervisor.

Communicating a Vision of the Future to the Supervisors/Middle Managers

A WCE implementation changes how everyone thinks and does their job, especially supervisors and middle managers. In a traditional company, supervisors perform some or all of the following duties:

♦ Make job/shift assignments

♦ Track factory or office output

♦ Set schedules

♦ Perform associate evaluations

♦ Hire associates

♦ Train associates

♦ Meet with customers

In WCE, these responsibilities are handed over to the production or office teams. If we have not properly communicated with the supervisors about what their role is in the future, they will begin, even if subconsciously, efforts to protect their jobs and prevent the hand-off of these responsibilities.

Make sure that all of these associates have a clear understanding of their options and career path in the future.

The 90-Day Rule

Once you have identified the WCE implementation "brickwall" disguised as the supervisor or middle manager, what is the next step? Apply the 90-day rule. This is when you sit down with this individual and review the company's reason(s) and urgency for the WCE implementation or "trip." Using the context of a trip, the discussion can go something like this: the company is going on a train ride to WCE. As a valuable member of our organization, you need to be on this train. To obtain a ticket to board this train for WCE, in the next 90 days there are specific new behaviors you must acquire, and specific old behaviors that must be left behind. A discussion, definition, and measures of the new and old behaviors then occurs. Follow up meetings, to discuss the progress in eliminating the old behaviors and adopting the new ones, are essential and scheduled (no less frequently than every two weeks). At 90 days, both parties should know what the decision on the boarding pass is.

If someone had asked us 25 years ago if everyone could change, we would have very optimistically said yes. Ultimately, our experience, supported by the literature, says no. What we need is to have open and honest dialogue with the identified brickwalls and present choices, options, and consequences.

Some people might be critical of the short length of time we recommend to adopt the new behaviors. Our experience has been that if people will not move seriously to adopting the new behaviors in 90 days, giving them six months or two years will not make any difference. The worst part is that, while they are not changing during this six-month to two-year period, these supervisors/middle managers can seriously disrupt your WCE implementation. Depending on their position and the size of the company, they might even cause it to become a program of the month.

Dealing with "brick walls" is difficult because some of these management associates were trained and promoted in the old "command and control" management style by the company. They could have even excelled at this style of management because, for them, being "in-charge" and telling people what to do was an ego or power trip.

Now we want them to support two-way communication, empowerment, visual communication and scheduling, and self-directed teams. We want them to learn how to coach and mentor. Making this conversion, from an 80s style that gave them raises and promotions, can be very difficult. To paraphrase Kotter, it's like telling someone to quit drinking, smoking, and go on a diet all at once.

Summary—Reason #3

There will be roadblocks, barriers, and brick-walls encountered on the WCE journey, and all of them will be people—management people. Remember to communicate, communicate, communicate to this group: the reason for WCE, how the business will change, and how their roles will change. Review the no-layoff policy. It applies to them also.

Prepare your version of the 90-Day Rule in advance of the brickwalls showing themselves (we can promise you there will be some). Act in a fair, honest, and timely fashion to avoid the high costs of stalling the implementation.

Improvement = Change

Business Insanity: Doing the same thing over and over and expecting different results.

#4 Not Understanding That This is About Your People

In the 1980s, when companies first starting feeling the pinch of foreign competition and the global economy, many of them thought that becoming World Class meant retooling their companies with automated equipment, robots, computers, and wire-guided vehicles. Eliminating people from the process was the goal. The term "lights out" operation was popular.

What these companies soon discovered, and what World Class companies already knew, was that equipment alone would not make them World Class. People with their skills, knowledge, and ideas were the key to improving processes. These companies, after spending billions of dollars on equipment, then found it necessary to scrap this equipment and retool with people.

People and the WCE Journey

So as we begin the journey to be a WCE, it is important to understand that World Class is accomplished:

- ♦ 80% through people

- ♦ 20% through techniques, equipment, and automation

Distinguishing Features of World Class Companies

Visiting World Class companies, for example, the Toyota plant in Georgetown, Kentucky, the Genie Industries plant in Redmond, Washington, or many of Dana Corporation's or Johnson Control's facilities, can be a very enlightening experience. While touring these facilities, people often describe the company environment as "different." The environment, or ambiance, is different in these companies because their focus is on people.

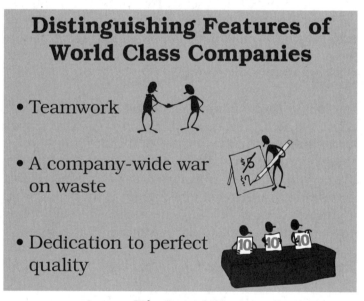

Distinguishing Features of World Class Companies

- Teamwork

- A company-wide war on waste

- Dedication to perfect quality

Figure 4-1

Figure 4-1 shows the distinguishing features of World Class companies. These features have a distinct people orientation.

First, teamwork is utilized throughout. Associates help each other. Again, the people in these companies understand that there are no individual winners or losers—they either win as a team or lose as a team. Many of these companies provide or offer a company uniform (a pullover shirt for example) to blur the differences between hourly and management associates, or different areas or departments.

The second feature is a company-wide war on waste. World Class companies make sure that all of their associates understand why becoming World Class is important to their customers, to the company, and to the individual associate. They train all associates to understand and identify parts of their process that the customer is unwilling to pay for (waste). They are also trained to use the waste elimination tools and techniques of WCE (Figure 4-2). With this training and associate empowerment in place, every associate in the facility is expected to make small waste elimination improvements every day.

Many companies start the WCE journey and say, "Do we really have to train *all* of our employees?" The answer, which was reviewed in Reason #1, is this: "Do you want 6-7 people improving the company—or all 400?"

It should be re-emphasized that the WCE tools and techniques shown in Figure 4-2 can be used by the 400 associates only if they work in an empowered environment. Again, the elements of an empowered associate are:

Impact of World Class Enterprise Techniques

■ = Significant Impact

World Class Enterprise Tools & Techniques

Typical Company Measurables	5S Visual Office & Factory	Problem Solving & Error Proofing	TPM - Total Productive Maintenance	Office or Manufacturing Cells	Setup Reduction	Enterprise-Wide Kanbans	Kaizen Events
Safety	■	■	■	■			■
Scrap/Rework		■	■	■	■	■	■
Inventory Turns	■		■		■	■	■
Unplanned Downtime			■				■
First Time Yield			■				■
On-time Delivery				■	■	■	■
PPM				■	■		■
Absenteeism	■	■		■			■
Sales Dollars Per Employee	■		■		■	■	■
Return on Assets	■		■		■	■	■

Figure 4-2

♦ Associates are recognized as the most valuable resource

♦ Teamwork is utilized throughout the organization

♦ Decision making is delegated to the lowest possible levels in the company

♦ Openness, initiative, and risk-taking are promoted

♦ Accountability, credit, responsibility, and ownership are shared.

The third feature of World Class companies is a focus on perfect product quality. All associates are responsible for the quality of the work they perform. World Class companies understand that the lowest cost way to produce any product or service is to do it correctly the first time.

Training as an Investment in WCE

The cost of training in traditional American companies is viewed as an expense. When business is down, and budgets or business plans are tight, training is usually the first line item that is cut. That is why, as was mentioned earlier, when some companies start the WCE journey, one of the first cost questions they ask is: Do we really need to train all of our people?

In World Class companies, training is seen as a required investment in the future. To again reference the *Industry Week* survey of companies that had a "significant" or "full implementation" of World Class manufacturing, 68.1% reported spending 2% or more of their labor budget on training. This compares to only 35.5% reported by the companies with "no progress" toward World Class. In terms of training hours, 46.7% of all companies reporting significant or full implementation trained all of their associates more than 20 hours per year. For no progress companies, this number was 18.8%.

The Industry Week data says this—associate training by itself will not make you World Class, but associate training is one of the required elements of the WCE implementation package that includes: top management support, good two-way communication, associate empowerment and participation, WCE goals and measurements, and a customer focus.

Summary—Reason #4

The associates in a company are the only vehicle management has to becoming World Class.

> **"The only strategic weapon a company has that can not be copied by the competition is its people, their focus, and their motivation."**
>
> George Koeninger

#5 *Lack of Customer Focus*

Customer Satisfaction Drives Profitability

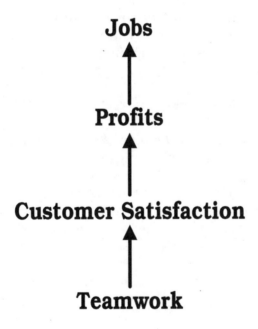

Jobs

↑

Profits

↑

Customer Satisfaction

↑

Teamwork

Figure 5-1

A simple model for competing in the global economy is shown in Figure 5-1. Starting with Customer Satisfaction, which is the only reason any company is in business, leads to company profitability. In fact, the companies which have the highest levels of customer satisfaction are also the most profitable. The Japanese have a wonderful saying: "Profits are the reward of the satisfied customer." When you think about it, this make a huge amount of sense. As consumers, don't we all frequent the businesses that satisfy us? If we get treated poorly at a place of business, we don't go back.

So customer satisfaction leads to profits which then leads to jobs. The reality is that companies are in the business of making money, not necessarily hiring people like us.

Teamwork Drives Customer Satisfaction

But where does customer satisfaction come from? It comes from teamwork, everyone pulling in the same direction. No blame games, no witch hunts, no "our department got it done but that other department screwed up and that's why we couldn't take care of the customer." Everyone is pulling in the same direction for the customer.

One of the nice things about focusing on customer satisfaction is that it is a common goal that everyone believes in and can pull toward. Remember, common goals build teamwork. Even the level-three gripers and complainers of Reason #3 understand that business is about taking care of the customer.

What is the definition of customer satisfaction? Widely used is this one: Customer satisfaction is meeting the customer's expectation for the quality, delivery, price, performance, and service of our part, product, or service. Some people would argue with this definition and say that the goal is to "exceed" the customer's expectation. Some people say the goal is to "delight" the customer. We agree with both statements, but there is a sequence: you must start with meeting the expectations—then you can move on to exceed and delight. For most companies, meeting the expectations is still the goal—especially now since those expectations change so frequently.

The idea that every associate in a business works for the customer is not a new concept. Eighty years ago, Henry Ford, Ford Motor Company, had an expression for this, shown in Figure 5-2. It is important that all associates understand that their paychecks come from the customer.

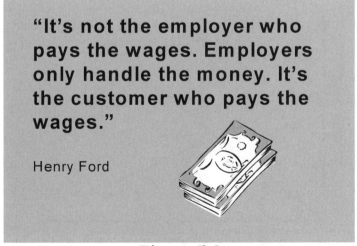

"It's not the employer who pays the wages. Employers only handle the money. It's the customer who pays the wages."

Henry Ford

Figure 5-2

The problem with most companies and customer satisfaction is that companies believe that doing more of what the customer wants will increase their business costs. Actually, the opposite is true. Companies misperceive the cost of customer satisfaction as shown in Figure 5-3.

Basically, customers are approaching all companies today saying they need better quality, lower prices, shorter lead-times, and better delivery. The reaction many companies have to these requests is to throw their arms up in the air and say, "How are we going to do all these things and still make money?" These companies believe that, as they increase levels of customer satisfaction, their costs will go up (as shown on the "perceived cost line" on Figure 5-3). The reality is that this is never, never, never true. Business costs always go down

The Cost of Customer Satisfaction

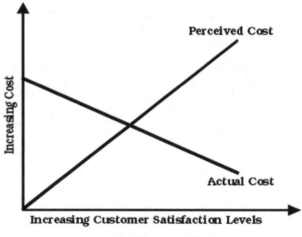

Figure 5-3

as customer satisfaction goes up as shown on the "actual cost" line.

Business Waste as a Roadblock to Customer Satisfaction

How is this true? The thing that makes our companies less competitive—business waste—is also the same thing that limits our ability to satisfy customers. To explain how this works we must define business waste:

Waste is anything other than the MINIMUM amount of people, time, equipment, material, parts, and space required to ADD VALUE to the product. To most everyone's shock and disbelief is the fact that most office and manufacturing processes contain up to 75% waste (Reason #10 will show how to test for this in your company).

We have introduced the term "adding value." It has two definitions. First, adding value is any operation or process the customer is willing to pay for. Second, adding value generally changes the "shape" or "form" of the part, product, service, or "information product." Office areas do not produce physical products, they produce "knowledge" or information products. Examples of adding value in manufacturing companies are machining, welding, painting, and assembling. Examples in the office are formatting a customer order so that it can be created in the factory or creating a customer drawing.

The problem with waste is that it hides in the woodwork or in the background. We have been doing wasteful activities for so long we think we need to do them. New processes are being developed today with waste designed into them. Figure 5-4 is a review of the eight general types of business waste.

8 General Types of Business Waste

Scrap/Rework/Repack/Recook/Corrections/Reconciliations

Transportation—Material handling or information "hand-offs"

Associate Motion—Non-value-added time such as looking for, searching, obtaining items such as prints, tools, materials, memos, files, reports, invoices

Associate Waiting Time—Non-value-added time such as waiting for materials, instructions, the supervisor, an e-mail, or a phone call

Inventory—Raw, work-in-process, finished

Overproduction—Producing more than the customer ordered

Overprocessing—Doing more than what the customer is willing to pay for

Underutilized Human Resources—The lack of involvement and participation of all the members of the workforce

Figure 5-4

Administrative Waste

Administrative waste is usually disguised as some of the items shown in Figure 5-5.

Conflicting Department Goals—Not everyone on the same page or pulling in the same direction

Traditional Accounting Methods—Rewarding people for creating waste, for example: excess inventory

Poor Product Designs—Designs which do not include the ideas and needs of both the internal (manufacturing) and external customer

Order Processing Time—In World Class companies, orders flow from the customer to the area that will produce the order

Searching, Hunting, Looking—For files, orders, invoices, reports, memos, supplies etc.

Waiting Time—For batched paperwork, a signature, instructions, the fax machine, a copier, a meeting to start or end on time, or the supervisor

Purchasing Reorders, Transactions, Supplier Invoices—Kanbans should be developed for all repetitive orders

Authorizations—The need for authorizations in a company is a big "red flag" signalling poor communication.

Figure 5-5

A classic example of hidden office waste is supplier invoices. Suppliers are required to set up an Accounts Receivable department and send invoices to customers, even though the customer's receiving department received and signed for the material. When the customer issues the purchase order for the material, the price of the item was known. Why force the supplier to supply invoices with information that is already known by the customer? Ultimately, the cost of maintaining an Accounts Receivable department at the supplier is borne by the customer—all waste!

Other disguised forms of business waste are shown in Figure 5-6.

Waste in U.S. Business is Usually Disguised as:

- Lost Time/Injury Accidents
- Machine Setups
- Machine Downtime
- 3rd Party Inspection – having someone inspect another person's work
- Receiving Inspection
- Inventory Storage
- Counting Inventory
- Supplier Lead-times
- Product Test–when it is accomplished only as a verification of the previous processes
- Other items camouflaged as work

Figure 5-6

Waste Elimination and Customer Satisfaction

When companies are asked whether there has ever been a circumstance in their company where scrap, rework, long machine set ups, or machine downtime have prevented them from making a shipment on time, or forced them into overtime or a premium freight situation, the answer is unanimously yes. We can begin now to see how business waste is a barrier which prevents us from taking care of our customers. Based on this fact, the entire focus of the tools and techniques of WCE is to identify and eliminate waste throughout the entire company. When we eliminate waste, we now know that two wonderful things happen to the company:

1. Business costs are reduced.

2. Automatically, and as an outcome of reduced business costs, the company is in a better position to satisfy the customer.

Summary—Reason #5

Focusing on the customer gives the company associates a common goal to rally behind. It becomes the basis for all the WCE improvement activities which can then make the company globally competitive, based on the needs of the marketplace.

Office Value-Added Processes

A process is a series of steps, operations, or procedures that the customer is willing to pay for. Adding value generally means changing the shape or form of the "knowledge or information product." If we listed all the steps, operations, or procedures on our invoice, the customer would be willing to pay for each of them.

#6 Lack of Improvement Measurements

Measure Only Those Things You Want to Improve

It is an axiom in WCE that you must set a baseline and have on-going measurements for any process you wish to improve. No baseline, no measurements—no improvement. Measurements are like maps. Maps can take you anywhere in the world that you want to go, but a map will do no good if you don't know where you are (the baseline).

But what do you measure? Companies make several big mistakes. First, companies make too many measurements. Some companies may measure 15-25 Performance Indicators (PIs) or Key Performance Indicators (KPIs). The reality is that people in most organizations can not successfully improve 15-25 items at one time because that is such an overwhelming number, for even the best people in the organization. It paralyzes everyone and, as a result, very little gets improved. This is especially true for associates on the shop floor who have just recently begun to experience an empowered environment where they can be involved and participate. When hit with these 15-25 numbers and asked for their help, they feel overwhelmed. A maximum of five items is suggested (more on this in Chapter 10).

Tie the Measurements into the Company's Goals

The second measurement mistake is that measurements are not directly tied to the company's budget or business plan goals. All measurements and improvement goals should support the company goals. As mentioned earlier, the WCE implementation should be designed around the current and future company goals that are usually outlined in the company's budget or plan. To enhance top management support, a World Class Enterprise implementation must positively affect these company goals quickly.

The third mistake is not setting office performance goals (assuming this ties back to the budget or business plan goals) for their "knowledge" or "information products" as part of the WCE implementation, and then not measuring office performance against those goals. Office areas have the greatest opportunity for productivity improvements because they have never been measured. Every manufacturing company can "spit out" what the shop floor productivity numbers are, but few can talk about office numbers.

Examples of both typical office and factory measurables are shown in Figures 6-1 and 6-2. Again the measurables must relate to the budget or plan.

Typical Office Measurables

- Safety
- Rework/Corrections of Customer Orders
- Time to Hire an Employee
- Time to Process Benefit Enrollment
- Productivity, Cost per Sales Order Produced
- Inventory Turns
- Time for a Financial at Month End
- Office Information Product Lead-Time
- # of Engineering Changes after a New Product Release
- Presenteeism
- Customer Complaints

Figure 6-1

Typical Company-Wide Measurables

- Safety
- Scrap/Rework
- Productivity
- Customer Quality
- Downtime
- Setup Time
- On-time Delivery
- Inventory Turns
- Supplier On-time Deliveries
- Supplier Lead-times
- Supplier Quality
- # of New Product Introductions
- New Product Development Time

Figure 6-2

Visually Communicate Measurements

On-going measurements, to affect change, should be displayed visually in the work areas. All members of the work area team should be able to see the measurements and fully understand them. Data should be recorded not less than hourly

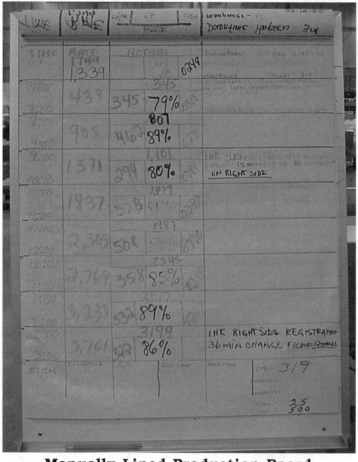

Manually Lined Production Board
Figure 6-3

for most processes. Top management should be able to walk throughout the company and see and understand how each area is doing against the goals, without asking a question.

Creating great ways to display the measurements is somewhat of an evolutionary process. It is suggested that you may start with a hand lined-out flip chart as shown in Figure 6-3.

Once we have the desired format, we can either have a template printed on the flip chart or create a lined out "white board" as shown in Figure 6-4.

PRODUCTION TRACKING BY SHIFT PER HOUR											
DATE: 3/29/00 **DP BUTTON**											
PART: 1024-0											
MACHINE: 50T											
CAVITATION: 2 **ASSEMBLY**											
STD. CYCLE TIME: 33.4											
CUMULATIVE 1ST				CUMULATIVE 2ND				CUMULATIVE 3RD			
HR	STANDARD	ACTUAL	COMMENTS	HR	STANDARD	ACTUAL	COMMENTS	HR	STANDARD	ACTUAL	COMMENTS
1	109	53	93 reject	1				1			
2	218	175	43 rej	2				2			
3	327			3				3			
4	436			4				4			
5	545			5				5			
6	654			6				6			
7	763			7				7			
8	872			8				8			

Template Production Board
Figure 6-4

The ultimate measurement—Real Time: an example is shown in Figure 6-5.

Real Time Production Board
Figure 6-5

Summary—Reason #6

Convert the company goals into process improvements. Measure any process that needs improvement.

#7 Lack of Lean Leadership

Managerial Leadership

The Dupont Company, considered by many to have World Class levels of safety in their facilities, uses the following expression to train its management people on safety, and to manage their facilities:

> *You will achieve the level of safety that you demonstrate you want to achieve!*

This Dupont expression applies to Dupont managers walking the safety talk, being the leaders, models, and examples of good safety practices.

We love this expression because not only do we believe it to be true for safety as Dupont has proven, but also it applies to all the tools, techniques, and improvements of WCE.

You will achieve the level of 5S, quality, productivity, teamwork (insert your desired improvement activity here) that you demonstrate you want to achieve!

It's not about telling the team what you want done—it's about showing them what you want done!

Lack of Lean Leadership—Two Real Examples

At the end of a report session for a 5S Kaizen event, the 5S team politely asked if upper management people could be involved in the next 5S event. In his office after the event, the general manager's comment to this request was "I'm not helping those damn people clean up their mess." Net result: end of WCE implementation (although it took about 6 months to die).

A small company trained all of its associates in 5S activities. A week later, several people noticed a supervisor walk over some trash on the floor, not stopping to pick it up. Net result: 5S was designated by the shop floor associates as another program of the month, which doomed it to failure.

Requirement for a Full-Time WCE Facilitator

For companies larger than 100 people, a full-time WCE facilitator is required. The WCE facilitator is the in-house "Lean expert." He or she does all the WCE training and is the "go to" person for kaizen event facilitation, questions, problems, and direction. Companies usually start this journey using outside consultants which is appropriate, although the company should designate and begin the development of its own expert (consultant) on day one. Becoming dependent on outside consultants will not make you World Class. After the WCE launch process is underway (first 6-9 months), consultants should be used only in monthly or quarterly initiative reviews.

For companies larger than 100 people, trying to implement WCE with a part-time facilitator does not work. Part-time becomes no-time.

Companies smaller that 100 people need a facilitator but this person can be a part-time facilitator (if necessary). In smaller companies, part-time works because everyone successfully wears multiple "hats" and the WCE work load is less.

The WCE Facilitator

A WCE facilitator is absolutely required for both the ongoing continuous improvement efforts and kaizen events. The facilitator is a necessary source of information which keeps the improvement efforts guided in the desired direction. This person facilitates but does *not* take responsibility for the improvement effort. The people who work in the improvement area must do that.

Ideally, as with any facilitator, this should be someone who is respected and trusted by everyone in the facility and has a strong desire to be a facilitator. This person should have excellent people skills and training skills, as well as kaizen event experience both as a participant and as an event leader.

We strongly believe the above noted facilitator skills require that the WCE facilitator be someone already in the company ranks. Hiring someone from the outside should only be done as a last resort.

Facilitator Responsibilities

This person facilitates communication and cooperation across cross-functional boundaries and is the resource for the following activities:

♦ Training—Provides a review of improvement information that the event team needs to make at the work site (for example, Setup Reduction or Kanbans). Updates the teams with new techniques or technology.

♦ Team developer—Clarifies team roles, goals, and decision processes. Builds team consensus. Helps teams overcome dispute and discipline problems from within and from outside the team. Keeps all lines of communication open.

♦ Coach/adviser—Helps the teams stay focused and on track. Makes sure the teams are measuring their own performance.

♦ Cheerleader—Sparks synergy and encourages the teams to be creative.

Also, for some length of time after a kaizen event has been completed, the facilitator follows up with the event area to make sure there are no event-related problems and that no backsliding has occurred. A highly people-skilled, knowledgeable, and organized facilitator is a prerequisite to successful WCE improvement activities.

In the company organization or reporting structure, the WCE facilitator should report dotted line to the top manager in the facility.

WCE Facilitator Development Programs

There are many companies and educational institutions offering "Lean Facilitator" certification programs. Their claim is to develop a facilitator in as little as a 3 to 10 days of classroom training. Be careful. If the goal is to develop an in-house expert/consultant, then 3 days to 10 days will not get you there! The best program at present appears to be the Lean Master Facilitator certification program offered by the Milwaukee School of Engineering (www.msoe.edu). MSOE has a complete offering of both classroom and shop floor (kaizen event) activities as part of the certification process.

Summary—Reason #7

A sustainable WCE implementation requires that top management are the leaders, models, and examples of the required behaviors for World Class success. In his leadership advice to top management about implementing business excellence, Tom Peters said it best: "They watch your feet, not your lips."

A successful WCE implementation also requires that the company develop an in-house expert who can live and help facilitate the changes and improvements.

#8 People Measures Not Aligned With WCE Goals

Requirements for Teamwork to Occur

Companies can make rapid WCE improvement progress when everyone is pulling in that direction as a team. But, how do you get that kind of teamwork? It starts with understanding the environmental elements in the workplace that support teamwork. As noted in Reason #2, these four elements are:

1. High levels of two-way communication throughout the organization.

2. Team members with diverse backgrounds.

3. Common purpose, motivated by mission. A strongly developed vision and mission for the organization helps all team members make the right decisions and saves time in the decision-making process. One has only to ask "Does this decision support the goals of the organization?"

4. Common goals, common measurements. Teamwork is enhanced when all team members understand the goals of the team and the organization, and has common mea-

surements, understood by everyone, to assess the progress made.

For purposes of this discussion, elements #3 and #4 are the topic (it assumes #1 and #2 are in place). In general, most organizations can successfully set common purposes and goals—their first choice being financial. In this case, we will assume there are WCE goals which are driving the financials. The problem is that most companies send conflicting messages to their associates in the WCE foundational areas of performance evaluations, promotions, rewards, and bonus systems. We want to implement WCE so we change and improve but we are trying to build WCE on performance evaluations, promotions, rewards, and bonus systems that were designed for a traditional business environment.

These conflicting messages can be used by the WCE brick walls and nay sayers to support their "Let's do it the way we have always done it" position. Here are the things that should be evaluated:

Performance Evaluations Based on Desired WCE Behaviors

Make sure management evaluations consider:

♦ Leadership, including being the model and example

♦ Communication activities (verbal and visual)

♦ Teamwork

♦ Commitment to continuous improvement using WCE tools and techniques

Supervisory evaluations should include:

♦ Development of coaching, mentoring, facilitating, and teaching skills

♦ Commitment to team based activities

♦ Teamwork

♦ Commitments to continuous improvement using WCE tools and techniques

Hourly associate evaluations should include:

♦ Commitment to and use of the continuous improvement tools and techniques of WCE

♦ Commitment to team based activities

♦ Teamwork

Promotions, Pay Increases, & Bonuses

Again, the goal is that no one gets promoted or financially rewarded unless they are leaders, participants, and contributors to the WCE implementation.

Promoting A Brick Wall Supervisor—A Real Example

A small manufacturing company (fewer than 100 people) started a WCE implementation. In the first year, the company made what it defined as good progress, even though its most senior supervisor did not support the WCE implementation. The improvements made in the first year could all be attributed to the efforts of the shop floor associates.

The supervisor was a classic example of the brick wall described in Reason #3—yes, yes, yes, in the meetings and training, then no, no, no, on the shop floor. When it was pointed out early on that this supervisor was an issue, top management, to a fault, was very loyal to this long-term associate. "He will come around, he will eventually understand." He didn't change and to our amazement eventually was promoted. The WCE implementation stalled and the improved processes actually reverted to what the supervisor, armed with a promotion, felt comfortable with. The associates on the shop floor quickly gave up and did what the supervisor told them to do!

Summary—Reason #8

To prevent sending conflicting messages and goals to your associates, align all systems in the company to the goals of the WCE implementation.

#9 Using Kaizen Events as the Sole Improvement Mechanism

Kaizen events are a powerful, team-based activity for making rapid improvements in an office or manufacturing process. Kaizen events can be focused on improving all the typical company measurables as shown in Figure 9-1.

Kaizen is a Japanese word that means to "change for the good." Doing "little things" better everyday defines kaizen—slow, gradual, but constant improvement in any area that will eliminate waste and improve customer satisfaction.

The Definition of Kaizen

Kaizen is what the Japanese did to the ideas they picked up from American manufacturers in the 1950s. The Japanese combined employee empowerment and kaizen and then had everyone in their plants doing "little things" better everyday. Kaizen is the most powerful tool in the Japanese manufacturing arsenal.

The target of kaizen is cost reduction through the elimination of waste at all levels in the business process.

The definition of kaizen has grown to mean

Impact of World Class Enterprise Techniques

■ = Significant Impact

World Class Enterprise Tools & Techniques

Typical Company Measurables	5S Visual Office & Factory	Problem Solving & Error Proofing	TPM - Total Productive Maintenance	Office or Manufacturing Cells	Setup Reduction	Enterprise-Wide Kanbans	Kaizen Events
Safety	■	■	■	■			■
Scrap/Rework		■	■	■	■	■	■
Inventory Turns	■		■	■	■	■	■
Unplanned Downtime	■		■				■
First Time Yield		■	■	■		■	■
On-time Delivery				■	■	■	■
PPM		■	■	■			■
Absenteeism	■		■	■		■	■
Sales Dollars Per Employee	■	■		■	■		■
Return on Assets	■		■	■			■

**Kaizen Event Impact on
Typical Company Measurables
Figure 9-1**

something different in American manufacturing. Most American companies do not recognize the potential of employee empowerment. American culture, in general, struggles with techniques that are gradual and produce small improvements— even if these small improvements occur daily! Americans are innovators and that means "giant steps." Home runs, not singles!

The difficulty is that companies that are in a "quick fix" mode inaccurately see and try to use kaizen events as the vehicle to make them World Class. Kaizen events may be the tires on that vehicle, but they are not the engine. All of the company's associates working together are the engine. Their knowledge, skills, ideas, and understanding of *why* the company is doing a WCE implementation keeps the engine running.

Events must be combined with the "Japanese kaizen" method of everybody making small improvements everyday for the WCE implementation to be successful.

What Can a Kaizen Event Accomplish?

A kaizen event will effect a rapid improvement in the performance of a specific project process, production process, office process, or manufacturing cell.

What a Kaizen Event Will Not Accomplish

♦ Long term change at the event work site. If events are used as the sole improvement strategy, backsliding will occur as soon as the event is over. Someone from the event team or the company's kaizen facilitator must monitor the work site on a daily basis and must continue to coach and counsel the team on the improvements and why they are necessary.

♦ A significant increase in the understanding of World Class Enterprise tools and techniques by the people who work daily in the event area. This applies when events are used as the sole improvement strategy.

♦ Changing the culture of the people who work daily in the event area

The reason events cannot accomplish the above activities is because of the short term, quick improvement nature of kaizen events. The reasons why the company is implementing WCE, overall company strategies, the company vision of the future, associate empowerment, etcetera, are not typically discussed. The participants in the event will receive training on what the event is trying to achieve, such as 5S, or setup reduction, and perhaps even team building, but after that, it's all about making the changes.

When Do You Use a Kaizen Event?

The optimum financial return from an event occurs when the kaizen is used in the pre-project/process planning stage. Use kaizen events to improve processes before the product goes into production. Work on improving the "proposed" process. Layout the office or manufacturing cell and simulate the process. Walk the process and conduct time studies. This is also an ideal time to make sure all tooling, fixturing, drawings, machines, and work instructions are accounted for and correct. Pre-production kaizens will result in:

♦ The lowest change implementation cost (versus after the product is in production)

♦ Reduced engineering or process changes after project/process begins

♦ An opportunity to orient and train all associates who interface with the process

♦ No addition to the project time

Unfortunately, most American businesses lack the vision of what this pre-production kaizen investment will do for the project launch/production costs, and only start to think about kaizen events after the project/process launches and there are quality, productivity, or other problems.

How Not to Use Kaizen Events—A Real Example

A Fortune 200 company with multiple facilities and in a quick-fix mode, hired a consulting company to help them implement WCE. After only a limited amount of communication to all its associates, they started doing only kaizen event improvement activities in their facilities. One event, the development of a manufacturing cell, was completed over a long weekend by a team that consisted of only the consultant and management people. When the equipment operators came to work on Monday morning, they were shocked, dismayed, and resentful that their area had been rearranged without understanding why, and without their knowledge or ideas. (All of us would feel the same way if this happened in our work area.) Lacking an understanding of why things were done, the operators, over time, then proceeded to try to put things back to the way they were comfortable with.

A year later, the consulting company and an estimated $1,000,000 in company money is gone. After closing several of its plants, the company is reevaluating its WCE effort.

Summary—Reason #9

Kaizen events are a powerful tool capable of making rapid business improvements. Kaizen events are only one element of the WCE implementation package that include: top management support, good two-way communication, associate empowerment and participation, WCE goals and measurements, and a customer focus.

#10 Bonus Pay Systems Where the Only Measure is Company Profitability

To clear up any confusion in Reason #10's title, companies can only pay bonuses when they are profitable! The *basis* from which bonuses are developed is where the problems exist.

In fact, we believe most companies are too meek about profitability. Companies have a right to a certain level of profitability determined by the amount of risk to the invested capital. Don't apologize for that! Without this right, everyone would just sell their businesses and put their money in a bank! Profit sharing—no! Gain sharing above the minimum expected level of profitability—yes!

The problem with bonus systems that are tied only to the level of profitability is that they do not teach the company associates how to link and align what they do to profitability. The reason no bonus was produced then becomes a finger pointing exercise because our associates do not know where profitability comes from.

Bonus System Goals

The goal of a bonus system is to align and link the company's goals and the associates' goals.

We must teach our associates cause (reduced costs) and effect (improved profitability), and then give them feedback on how they are doing at least hourly (see Reason #6, measurements). Our associates will make us World Class: we just need to give them the training, tools, goals, and measurements.

In Reason #1, we noted that this is the formula in the global economy that determines company profitability:

Profit = Selling Price - Cost

The selling price is now set by the customer/consumer. Companies now can control profitability by controlling their costs.

Reduced costs are one of the outcomes of a WCE implementation. Bonuses should therefore be tied into the organization's cost drivers. The actual bonuses should be funded by the reduction or elimination of cost drivers (convert all drivers into dollars). Which cost driver you work on first is identified or tied back to the company budget or business plan as discussed in Reason #6. Some potential cost drivers are shown in Figure 10-1.

Bonuses Should Focus on and be Funded by Cost Drivers:

- Safety
- Scrap/Rework
- Rework/Corrections of Customer Orders
- Office Information Product Lead-Time
- Productivity
- Customer Quality
- Downtime
- Setup Time

- Cost per Sales Order Produced
- Inventory Turns
- Supplier On-time Deliveries
- Supplier Lead-times
- Supplier Quality
- Product Development Time
- On-time Delivery
- Cost per Supplier Invoice

Figure 10-1

Remember, two of the prerequisites for teamwork are common goals and common mission. If bonuses are to be used to align the company's goals and the associates' goals, it must be a team activity. Either everyone earned a bonus or nobody earned a bonus.

Considerations in Developing a Self-Funded Bonus Plan

♦ Start the bonus system during the second year of the WCE implementation to avoid distractions while associates are learning about the tools and techniques of WCE.

♦ Associates should know what the company's expected level of profitability is.

♦ Select a maximum of five cost drivers that will be measured and tracked.

♦ Start with an 80 (company) -20 (associates) dollar split on reductions produced. Reduce to 50-50 as improvements are made.

♦ Payouts should be a maximum of quarterly while still protecting the company's right to profitability. Hold backs to protect company profitability are okay.

♦ If a bonus system is already in place, this system should give the possibility of a greater payout.

♦ In the 4th-6th year of the bonus, the system will have diminished many of the cost drivers. It may be necessary to switch at that time to a "gain sharing" system.

♦ Keep an up-to-date posting of the bonus status.

What's the Bonus Opportunity?

Here is the neat part–what the possibilities are for the bonus system and improvements for the company. In Reason #5, we noted that most office and manufacturing processes contain up to 75% waste. Most people find this difficult to believe. Figure 10-2 shows how companies can measure their "value-added" pie. It represents the results of video taping a person in a company for an entire day/shift. The next day, sit down with that person and segregate the activities they performed

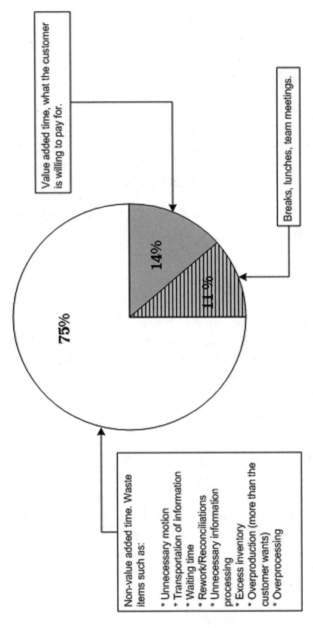

Figure 10-2

on the video. From the video we see that 11% of their day was spent on breaks, lunches, 5S time, and in team meetings. That part we are happy with. We want them doing those activities.

The next part of the pie, 14%, was spent adding value, doing things the customer was willing to pay us to do. The rest of the day, 75%, was spent on non-value added activities—things the customer will not pay us to do.

But if the customer will not pay us to do these wasteful activities, who does? The company, and it's coming right out of profits and potential bonuses!

The goal of WCE and the bonus system is to convert all waste into value-added time so the pie looks like Figure 10-3. Remember that the productivity improvements that come with WCE are a result of working smarter–not harder. We are eliminating the wasteful things people are doing and substituting things the customer will pay them to do.

Need to Chase Low Wages?

For the last several years, newspapers have been filled with articles about companies moving to Mexico and China and then exporting their products back to the U.S. These companies say they can't compete while paying U.S. wages. In general, this doesn't make sense to us.

For these companies, if the current company pie looks like Figure 10-2, don't we have huge op-

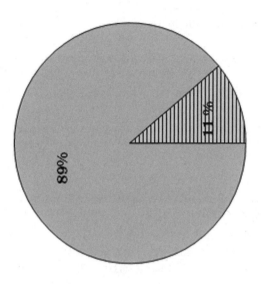

To value-added time:

Potential Productivity Improvement
Available as Business Waste is Eliminated
Figure 10-3

portunities for productivity improvements? If we are paying our people $15.00/hour and we increase value-added time from 14% to 28%, isn't that effectively cutting the wage rate in half? Then we could go from 28% to 56%. Again, in half! What are the possibilities in your business?

Now if your value-added pie already looks like Figure 10-3, then maybe chasing low wages is the answer.

Bonuses as Entitlements—A Real Example

The owners of a small company (less than 200 people) that did well for many years, gave out bonuses every year just because they wanted to share the good fortunes of the company with all the associates. The owners didn't tie the bonuses to profitability or any measure the associates might relate to. When business declined and the owners felt that giving out bonuses would be a hardship on the company, there was an uproar from the associates: "Where are our bonuses, we deserve our bonus," with absolutely no regard for how the company was performing.

Summary—Reason #10

A well-designed bonus system can quickly align company and associate goals to target your WCE implementation to the needs of business budget or plan.

Bibliography

"2003 Census of Manufacturers: Executive Summary." Industry Week/ Manufacturing Performance Institute. 2003.

Kotter, John. *Leading Change.* Boston: Harvard Business School Press, 1996.

Rubrich, Larry, and Mattie Watson. *Implementing World Class Manufacturing: Business Manual.* 2nd ed. Fort Wayne: WCM Associates, 2004.

Scannell, Edward E. and John W. Newstrom. *The Complete Games Trainers Play: Experimental Learning Exercises.* New York: McGraw-Hill, 1994.

Solomon, Jerrold M. *Who's Counting? A Lean Accounting Novel.* Fort Wayne: WCM Associates, 2003.

Taninecz, George. "Long-Term Commitments." Industry Week, *Feb. 2004: 51-54.*

Index

C

S

Safety 38, 85
  Lost-Time Accidents 41
Selling Price Formula 11
Setup Reduction 98
Standardized Work 36
Suppliers 5
  Quality Problems 40

T

Team Leader 40
Teamwork 24, 70, 88, 91, 103
  Common Goal 77
  Diversity 30
  Elements Necessary to Occur 29, 91
The Dupont Company 85
The MPI Group 10
Top Management Support 5
  Enhancing 80
Toyota 64
Toyota Production System 1, 5
Training 67, 88, 99
  Results 67
Trust 18

U

Unions 32, 57
United Technologies 32

V

Value-Added 15
Value-Added Time 106
Vision of the Future
  Communication to Middle Managers/Supervisors 59
Visual Communication
  A Visitor can Tell What's Going On 50
  Examples of 47

W